www.fast-print.net

The Naked Goddess
Copyright © Jeanette Slavinski 2012

ISBN 978-178035-269-5

First published 2012 by
FASTPRINT PUBLISHING
Peterborough, England.

Acknowledgements

THE
Naked
GODDESS

The Naked Goddess is dedicated to HelpforHeroes.

*There are many wonderful people far & wide who have helped to launch this anthology & deliver it to the world.
I want to thank the brave heroes who helped initiate its conception, without their prowess & bravery on the battlefields our universe would be far from safe for us & future generations to live in.*

Special thanks to The Vatican, Pope Benedict XV1. BBC Radio Lancashire, John Gillmore Show, who believed in my project & continuously helped broadcast its content. Simon Briggs of Stonehurst Estates for help with promotion & printing cost. Bluebird Bus company, Antonio Franchitti of Indulgence, who faithfully stayed with me on the project from the start alongside Simon Jakes. Judy Jakes, MGN design for their web design. Lt. Norman Hariss & Lance Corporal Tyler Christopher. My late father, Sargeant P. Slaven who taught me the fine principles of Pelmanism. Don Wilson for his dulcet tones & splendid help hosting our promo soireé in the presence of, The Lord Mayor of Manchester.

And of course my beloved Mum, Daniel & Gabrielle who put up with my continuous poetry recitals & for giving me endless encouragement.

Jeannette
Slavinski x

THE NAKED GODDESS

Photograph - Linda Pelling

"There is a poem in the heart of every human being"

Jeannette Slavinski

A reality anthology "for the people by the people"

Contents

Young poet laurate

WELCOME TO THE NAKED GODDESS

L ate 2010 an idea to share an anthology with the Nation in support of Help for Heroes was conceived, as Jeannette Slavinski's own mantra believes, "Everyone has a poem in their heart". A name was chosen, The Naked Goddess, a metaphor to capture imaginations.

In the local village, of Bramhall's Bistro, Indulgence, the baptism was shared & The Naked Goddess's ideology embraced the web & became www.thenakedgoddess.com in support of Help for Heroes, incorporating BBC Radio, Facebook & other media channels.

The word had been spoken, freestyle poetry flowed in under the themes of Love & War from around the globe, hearts & minds had been ignited & the anthology had become a reality book, For the People by the People, As one of England's finest actors, Timothy West. CBE. Endorsed the books idea, followed by aristocratic socialite Tara Palmer Tompkinson's own ditty.

WHY HELP FOR HEROES?

As part of The Lancashire Fusiliers & Royal Artillery, Jeannette's late father, Sargeant Peter Slavin served in the British Army for 32yrs as a gunner during WW11.

From an invite to meet former Mayor of Carmel, California & film star Clint Eastwood, The Goddess's artful idea was beginning to manifest rapidly. Deeply inspired by her fathers Military action & Clint Eastwood's stance as Mayor of Carmel & Military stand plus the magnetism of Carmel, the ink flowed narratively, encouraging the opportunity of sharing such amazement & blessing with the world & injured service men & women of war.

A further invitation to World Book Day 2011 opened another chapter as Byrchall High School, improvised a workshop around, The Making of The Naked Goddess, encouraging the teenage students to pen their own verse. With great delight & honour a Young Poet Laureate sections was then included.

Journeying further afield, the wheels on the Bluebird Bus turned round & round as Veteran Lt. Norman Hariss & Jeannette promoted patriotic roses & poetry on Valentines Day, whole heartedly welcomed by amused passengers.

The whole conception to help support Help For Heroes was finalised after Joe Christopher submitted a poem and letter about his son Lance Corporal Tyler Christopher who was severely injured in Afghanistan. In the face of adversity Tyler continues his heroic deeds for Help for Heroes, Wounded Warriors & supports The Naked Goddess. With great admiration The Naked Goddess collaborated with an American music producer who agreed to mix a US veterans donated poem to music, which includes lyrics about Help for Heroes & Wounded Warriors.

Ceasar had perished from the world had not his sword been rescued by his pen.

(HENRY VAUGHEN).

Unarmed combat

By David O'Leary

He yearns to return to Afghanistan,
To the dust & the heat & the cold.
He'd go because his real friends are there,
Light hearted, amusing yet prodigiously bold.

He yearns to return to Afghanistan,
To the dangers, the hardships, the trials.
He'd go because he was part of it,
His rejection still rankles; it riles.

He yearns to return to Afghanistan
To that bare earthen desert, sans charm.
He'd go because he left of him there.
His soldier's right arm!

You are not alone

By Gaynor Grimshaw

Absence makes the heart grow fonder
But it is a painful track
Every day, I pray & wish,
That I could have you back.
I kiss your picture every night
Talk to your photo frame,
Tell you all my ups & downs
& call you by your name.
I've saved the gifts from Xmas time,
Easter & Valentines too,
Can't wait to celebrate
All of these special times with you.
I know you've had a hard time
You're tired & missing home
But I wanted to write
And let you know,
That you are not alone.

100th

By Colin Miller

November 25th 2010 another sad day
Grieving people with their respects they pay
Uncontrollable tears fall to the ground
Engines of cars the only sound
The lucky ones salute, the Hurst's full of Red
He was twenty two a whole life ahead
The one hundredth life to be lost this year
For his family & friends no Christmas cheer
Lets not forget those who have paid the ultimate sacrifice
Lets not forget those who have paid the ultimate price
Forever in his grave forever he will lay
November 25th 2010 another sad day.

Hoi Poloi

BY. Michael Burgess.

If Clare was there yes anywhere that place I know would be more fair
She is a breath of fresher air her thoughts are deep her kind is rare
At first I missed it now I bear the shame of blindness to the glare
Of what was hidden now laid bare she dares to dream and dreams to dare
Now hear my mind let me declare though hoi poloi may stand and stare
If I was trapped within her lair my heart would float and not despair
For but to joy would I be heir I'm sure I'd know contentment there
Her will is iron and gold her hair, her name means brightness that is......Clare.

Their time is now

By Bette Braka

Their time is now,
They gave a vow,
They lived through trouble and strife,
They gave their life.
Other's have given their arms & legs,
Returning home to their children & wives
Wondering how the future will be,
Will they be able to maintain their family?
In some cases their minds are blown,
Nightmares day & night,
All because they went to fight.

Instead of an Army Division,
What about the Premier League Division?
One week's salary would never be missed.
There would be no pain,
But what a gain!!
Terry, Gerrard, Lampard, Ferdinand,
Lead the Band.
Show that charity comes from the heart,
Make a start!!
Forget the Roar of the Crowd,
See in the eyes of the injured & bereaved
That your compassion can be believed.
Remember when you go out to play
You always live to fight another day.

Memory

By Tara Palmer Tomkinson

A contact in my phone,
A picture in a frame,
But you will always be
A memory in my heart.

For all the years

Anonymous

To my love
For all the years I've loved you so,
For all the times we'll always know,
For every moment of pure joy,
Your gift to me to enjoy,
To the end of time my love,
You will be mine my love,
Fired by the joy of life,
Together we are the force of life
Transcending all temporary strife.
All the dreams we make come true
All the years I've lived for you
For my husband you belong to me,
Like the caressing breeze that flows free,
It's you and me for eternity.

Old Tommy

By Anthony Mcmaster

Have you seen old Tommy sitting in his wheelchair
No-one seems to notice him, no-one seems to care
He just sits there mumbling but no-one seems to listen
No-ones even interested, no-one knows he's there.

He won't wear his medals says they're just old metal
Doesn't need to wear them to remind him of the war
Says he's not a hero it was just part of his duties
Of the men he saved that day most have passed away

And have you seen the Colonel marching through the garden
Knees up high against his chest a salute for everyone
Dressing gown for a trench coat wellies for his boots
Every time it thunders his walking stick he shoots.

Libya

By Maureen Brindle

You vaporize my heart with a missile attack,
People circling round in a wild pack,
Tanks in a twisted metal stack,
Justice and freedom is the cry,
Control of oil, land, sea & sky,
How many people have to die?
Hearts & minds can no longer be heard,
Freedom is a meaningless word,
Without life it is absurd.
To interfere without understanding,
To make war without forward planning,
To kill with the intention of saving,
Tracer bullets over an illuminated palm tree,
Bomb craters near the Mediterranean Sea,
What is the deadly price of being free?

Buy a bloody poppy

By Joe Christopher

Last year was a painful one, where I watched my son and others suffer.
But these boys and girls are not like us, they're made of something tougher.

Their pains are forever, the deaths can't be undone.
We complain about the cold, they simply crack on, and on.
Those, alive & dead, are an example of living life,
So question your next argument, no ones died, no limbs lost,
everyone survives.
On our breast is a scarlet thought, that must never be forgot.

War is an abattoir. Romantic it is not.
My black skin, & your free thought would not exist but for them.
Boys ground to sausage meat; women blown to hell.
In fields of Flanders, Dunkirk's Killing beach, with sand like bloody tar.
Baghdad stinking corridors, & the thieves of Lashkar Gar.

You dont need to be Christian on Sunday to remember
The boys that should be old men this autumn; this November.
It aint necessary to believe in God, on the eleventh at eleven.
Give a minute for the soldiers who gave & who are still giving

Rest in peace you who've died, your loss was not in vain.
God be with you who have survived, may time ease your pain.
My scarlet thought is a little thing, no more than a little red button.
Its just a way to say that none of you will ever be forgotten

Next time you think that your waters have become very dark & choppy.
Works to hard & unfair & colleagues efforts sloppy,
And home life is uncomfortable & making you unhappy.
Stop & contemplate your luck,
Understand how safe we are, &

BUY A BLOODY POPPY!

Another poppy

By Jeannette Slavinski

Bleeding & broken
You lay bare,
In the bullet wasteland
Of despair.
Who can condone
your silent groan?
Another poppy
Sown far from home.

Life

by Lillian Gertrude

Life is such a precious gift
Live it while you may,
For the seconds just like raindrops
Fall & run away.
Fill it full of purpose
Every minute of the day,
For on the road of no return
We pass no more this way.
The thread of Life is fragile
When broken, cures are sought,
Though money can buy many things,
Life cannot be bought.

Love hate and war

By Courtney Hayles

How do I love you?
When this war of words outstretched across this
Battlefield continues into the early hours,
Breaking day smiles by shattering
The space to breathe & misunderstanding it for a reason to leave...
Leave me be! I dived into the bunker where I could gain scope on this
Love Hate War from a distance.
Yet your persistence to fight off, what was left of what might have
been... could have been...
Leaves me with no option but to submit my peace treaty,
Readily assembling army troops to ascend on your fortified walls
Of not interested in what I have to say.

I pray that you'll sway through spotlight interrogation...
That you'll look to the light & see that this pressure weighing you
Down isn't my way of stopping from uttering sound,
Sounds from my foolish actions that did happen from splitting the
fractions of seconds...
I tried to calm you down but we remained embroiled in deadlock,
Chained to our seat outlasting the words of defeat...
All of this because trivial accusation turned its back on my hearts will
To fill the wound your eyes did bleed me with...
There has to be a way...

I apply gorilla warfare tactics, tracking your thought paths over foreign
Terrain, placing wit against the grit of your teeth, pulling at your ropes of
false Hope... I'm helpless...

But First to your aid to Trade all of the above for Love.

Lost love

By Maggie Kvasnik

I can't believe the love we had
Could ever slip away
Yet here we are alone & sad
The price we have to pay
Your love was strong but I was weak
I never meant to stray.

I know in time the hurt will go
Some wounds will surely heal
But deep inside the scars are there
That you and I must feel
And oh how tender are they now
So new, so raw, so real.

I'd like to think we will be well
And love will grow anew
We both deserve some mercy now
Some peace is surely due
An antidote to constant pain
Is what I wish for you.

Victory

By Linda Walsh

The war is now over, the war has been won,
Its down to our troops & what they have done,
God bless all our lads, and all our girls too,
Kuwait is now free and its all down to you,
Our prayers have been answered,
Our dreams have come true
The war is now over and its victory to you.

Their victory was gallant
Their victory was bold
Their victory of war will always be told,
So to all of our troops, and allies as well
Your victory of war we're so proud to tell.
Soon all our troops will return back from war.
Back home to their families and loved one's once more,
Everyone will celebrate & shout out their praise
The lads are our heros & hats off they'll raise
Three cheers for our forces, we'll hear people shout,
Three cheers for our allies for they helped us out.
We'll all praise their victory when they return home,
Knowing their loved ones are now not alone.
So to all our forces, we'd like to say

WE'RE SO PLEASED TO CHEER YOU ON
YOUR VICTORIOUS DAY.

All the church bells ring

Anonymus

All the church bells will ring,
All the song birds will sing,
The sun will shine on your day,
And all the people will pray,
That your marriage will bring you joy,
As we all remember a brave boy,
Who became the People's Prince.
He joined the troops in Afghanistan,
And always does what he can.
This will be such a happy day,
All Britain will say
People & Monarchy can be proud,
Rejoicing people, cheering crowd
And heaven will bless from above,
Prince and Princess with enduring love

Who will remember me?

By James. A. Brown

Not long now
I'm not frightened, just alone, & lonely
Who will remember me?
The things I have done,
Things I have been happy about,
& sad about?

Girls I have loved, & lost,
Memories like the smoke that glides
Across the bodies of fallen comrades,
Silent now, and for all time

Who will remember me?
I am cold, so cold, not long now
My family will remember me, how I love them all,
And how I have missed them all
I love them, I love them, oh dear god how I love them
Lord of hosts, forgive my sins, let me see them again,
Let this love not die, here, with me
Oh my Lord God...will you remember me?

What a wonderful thought

Phyllis Ing aged 99

Wouldn't it be wonderful
If all the world were at peace
And all fighting, killing & hatred
Did really end & truly cease.
Wouldn't it be wonderful
If no more children died
From starvation & diseases
Because no one really tried,
To help and teach their parents
The best way how to live,
And how to prevent diseases.
Just a little time to give.
Wouldn't it be wonderful
If every child could go to school
And learn about each other
That hate is out & friendship is the rule.
Wouldn't it be wonderful
If famine was no more.
And bombing and destruction
Were gone for evermore.
Wouldn't it be wonderful
If our grandchildren & their children too
Were able to spend their lives in peace
Which we have failed to do.
I cannot see the world at peace
As time is fleeing by
For I am getting on in years
Having reached the age of ninety five.
But wouldn't it be wonderful
If every nation got together
And began to learn & understand
The ways of one another.

Eclipse

By Anthony Bray

As the middle of the day turns black as night,
Encumbered by the body of our satellite
On a Cornwall coast grew a tremendous crowd,
At the encroaching presence of the lunar shroud.
Excitement and tension finally comes to grips,
As the Luna cascades her black satin gown
Forty minutes to noon on the epoch count down.
Manchester's cloudy curtain has shrouded the light,
Obscuring the moment of this spectacular sight;
Not as dramatic as Cornwall in total pitch black,
The sensation of the moment by no means did lack.
For a few moments, the sky was tangible, dark ink,
This wonderous spectacle makes you sit and think;
As the suns bright corona is finally unfurled,
Bringing brightness & beauty to this awe inspired world.

The Royal Wedding

By Dorinda Mcdown

An April heat wave set the scene,
For the couple who will be King and Queen.
The entire world came to cheer,
The happiest day of the year.
Westminster Abbey was bedecked with trees.
The Royal couple before God on their knees.
For love & duty their heads bow,
Affirming their sacred vow.
Kate's dress a simple web of lace,
The bride elegant, poised & fair of face,
The epitome of loveliness & grace.
The Abbeys' bells pealed,
And a couple's love was sealed.
Prince William was resplendant in uniform of brightest red,
Our Prince saluting with his Princess dutifully bowing her head
In an open coach to the Palace balcony for kisses;
Greeting the seas of cheering crowds with good wishes.
A comical policeman cheers the people on,
And an appearance from a reluctant sun.
A cartwheeling verger down the Abbey's solemn aisle,
Made the whole world smile.
Loyal subjects thank Her Majesty,
For giving us her dynasty.
Her wedding bouquet Princess William gave,
For the Unknown Soldiers' Westminster Abbey grave.

Camouflage

By Robert. M. Sorensen

Making my way through a Vietnam Jungle. Passing the corpses of the
Bleeding in slumber. Choppers search for the insurgent crews.
Mount an offence before a defense brews. Angel of death has no favorites.
Centuries of torment & resourceful theft. All we know is to hold on,
& steal, Bomb and parade. Napalm spreads like the devil rampaged.

Walk through the flames, dry ice burns, too. Leeches & ticks will
Suck you dry to the bone An American Hero soon to be outcast once you
Return home. Every day is Christmas, Napalm tropical snow showers....
Every 24 hours, The military anti-Genesis. The devil's laughter
Echoes in screams that are silent. Turning Asian Tribes from hardcore
Reds... beached dying jellyfish.

Kill the opponent, stick it in good! Pray that you live until tomorrow,
Repenting to God will never end your sorrows. Spare the rod, inject the needle,
Smack soothes the head, & kills the fever. Tumbling dominoes fall
In all directions, Magnetic forces reverse this action.

The sacred goddess mountain

By Jeannette Slavinski

She sits
Waiting silently
Amidst a choir of cloudy tailed chariots.
Deity in disguise.
She is your Nathola Mustang Maya,
A seismic personality
With eyes like nipples, piercing
Enticing, emancipating you if,
You are brave enough to mount her.
She is
Love & War.
Draped in a virginal sari
Forever kissing her feet,
She awaits impatiently her eruption.
Shimmying, shuddering,
Sequined as an ice-maiden
In snowflakes
Waiting for her thaw,
Her law is mandatory.
Dominatrix, demanding, denying you,
Challenging your mettle as you smell
Her blood set in stone,
The bedrock hidden beneath
Her ice core.
You need to conquer her heart.
Lard yourself with lineament before you try,
One false move
And you die

As you hear her mesmerizing
Orifice mysteriously, whispering Newari.
Her crevasses of frozen waterfall tears
Bewitch your slippery thirst
As she vaporises into a mist of manna,
She is
The tease,
The nectar you need
That will poison your frenzied thoughts
If you fail this temptress.
Like Queen Devaladevil,
She has the power to quake you
Wake the Genghis in you.
Her word is hushed
Mark her
For she is unclaimed
As Everest Kingly,
Gazes behind her.

Abstract picture by Arturo Rhodes

#

By Rich. D. Hughes

Please Sir, don't leave me to die in this trench,
Which is empty of life but alive with the stench
Of my comrades who've fallen, like fodder for cattle
Please Sir I beg, Take me to the battle

Please Sir, I ask let me go with the boys
Over the top and to hell with the noise
One final attack will release me from pain
I swear Sir I shan't be returning again

Please Sir I pray , don't let me die here
In this squalor and slime , frozen by fear
Deaf from the noise and blinded by blood
Don't leave me to die in these trenches of mud

Please Sir, Assist me in loading my gun
Fix up my bayonet - let me at the hun
My festering wounds do not give me much time
Allow this proud soldier to die on the line...

Thoughts of a brave hero, I never knew

By Jenny Wrenn

I tread on golden leaves
Autumn is here, at home
I have melancholy thoughts of a Hero –
Was he sad & alone?
The trees are now cold and bare
Winter is here with an ice packed heart
A Hero from the past world
Is now, too far apart
To speak; To say
Where he has been
What he has seen

But I did not know him anyway

And now he lies in his honoured Soldier's Grave
A Hero I never knew; just someone so brave

Nuclear war impending

By John Farmer (Former England & Stoke City player)

Invade not ever or worse will be
In every peaceful day,
Devised in mans unsettled mind
Polluted in his way.
Ponder now then meditate
Until you see a sign,
Rest your body while you breathe
Naked in your kind.
Your axe of wroth must never fall
Upon this fertile soil,
Your devils spade must not be turned
Among such honest toil.
The implements that ply your trade
The carnival that rides,
The sites and submarines we've built
To swim the salt sea tide.
Your pretence of goodness in this day
Does outweigh the fears,
The impending terror in your grasp
Can only bring us tears.
The theory's justifying your being
& harvest ripe in stone,
The sorrow of your day is nigh
Should we ever go to war?
Yet will your value be outgrown?
And if it will how long
Or will your grip soon be replaced,
By one who's stronger?

But for the time rest in peace
If peace is what you bring,
Yet if your whip is cracked just once
The chords of fear will ring.
Still our rainbows forming yet awhile
The futures ours yet still,
Thank God you've never struck in haste
Pray God you never will.

S.O.S.

Mrs. M.C.Doherty

I lost my baby yesterday -
I cannot bear the pain
I look around & call and call
But sadly, all in vain.

The men, they came & killed her
And all the others too
Just three weeks' old, so soft and white
Now what am I to do?

So brutal were these monsters
They dashed her to the ground
Her soft head hit the hard ice flow
And blood lay all around.

Please tell the people of the world
To leave us seals in peace
Don't use our babies for your coats.
This killing has to cease.

Peace has to be more ...

By Beverly Sellen

Peace has to be more than the absence of war
For the absence of war is simply a truce
Till the men of violence find an excuse
To fight.

Peace has to be more than the absence of war
For the making of peace has to challenge and stop
Injustice and prejudice from its roots right up
To full height.

The making of peace has got to be more
Than a passive response to the making of war
The making of peace takes effort and skill
& tears and sweat & a steadfast will
To bring people together who'd much rather kill
Than talk & resolve & forgive & build
& unite.

Peace has to be more than the absence of war
To make peace every person must play their part
Not passively wait for another to start
For the making of peace must begin in my heart
As an act of will overcoming the dark
To bring light.

Last battle

By Alan Mckean

Sitting quietly in his favourite chair
A glass of wine alongside
He ponders his last battle.

Memories stand before him,
On parade
Just like his old regiment,
How many years ago?

He remembers his comrades,
Their support for him,
His support for them,
In those dark 1940's days.

So many battles
So many lost friends
So many laughs
So many tears.

His young wife,
So many years ago,
Now gone,
Her battle lost a few years back.

Their children
And theirs,
Now call round weekly
To check on the old man.

He remembers the early years
& the daily struggles
For even basic needs.
So many empty political promises.

Soldiers,
Forgotten & tossed aside,
Disillusioned by politicians.
He fears for today's soldiers.

The daily climb
Up the ladder of respectability
Hard, but rewarding.
Each rung a personal milestone.

Save a penny here,
Save a penny there.
Buy only what you can afford
Becomes their credo.

The daily hope
That your children
Will fare better
Than you.

His mind drifts again,
Back to his army days,
& friends long gone.
He still sees young faces.

His old fashioned values
Are now derided
"Out of date, "Out of touch" and "Out of time"
Say the Thought Police

His pension dwindles,
His memories merge.
He longs for other days,
When the battle lines were clear-cut.

He knows
That his last battle approaches.
He knows
He will not win this one.

He's alone, but not lonely.
He's got all his memories to remember
For one last time,
Until his young wife comes for him again.

My grandads' first world war

By Maureen Brindle

He lied about his age & volunteered to fight,
His shoes packed to increase his height.
With his Scottish poets' name, he went to war,
Patriotism was what he was fighting for.

Now a machine gunner in France,
With a mule & a heroic chance,
Six O' Clock aim & ordered to kill,
Raw swedes from the field his belly to fill.

Forward they went, forward they fought,
Distant the deaths the machine gun brought,
His grandma came to say goodbye,
He knew the exact moment at home she did die.

Home would never be the same again,
One more sadness amid the pain,
But for all those who died,
All his life a tear he cried.

For the German boy over the trench he came,
And killing him was not the same.
"It was either him or me,
But the difference between us was hard to see."

At last on a troop ship home,
Unconscious with pneumonia amid'st the foam,
The ship to Ireland was sent,
No victory march just mal intent.

Home to England civvies won,
Now his army days were gone,
In his brides' eyes the future shone,
& he was only twenty-one.

The naked goddess

By Jeannette Slavinski

My mother's wordy womb,
Olympic oracle
Embellishes volumes -
Poetry in motion.
Two hearts in one
Enriched, forever -
Pulsating bleeding beats.
Harnessed by her power
Loving nutrient -
I`m vitalised, nourished
An Umbilical chrysalis.
I hear music, its language
My adopted note,
Celebrating my soul
Ghostly dancing
In a gossamer Elysium

Turbulently I'm stripped
Violently charioted,
Into a contracting inferno,
A monochrome darkness
Of volcanic eruption,
A bruised vortex
From whence I`m delivered, Naked.
Inhalation, exhalation, exclamation,
Exposed, expressed Muse,
Waxing lyrically, I'm alive.
Rooting for the taste
Of alabaster milk.
Alchemist of natures love
The Naked Goddess.

Ink of love

by Carla James

My letters were written in ink of love.
I'd sit & write to ease his plight, my soldier brave, whose daily fight
Made my soul swell, each word would tell
Him how much pride there was inside.
He'd let me know how each love note arrived in
Places so remote, not just in terms of distant places
But also in warm, love filled spaces
To bring him joy every time
His eyes did read those words of mine.
On his camp bed my notes were read
Our miles apart were none he said
The ink of love, our magic potion, closed the gap
By sheer devotion from his sweetheart's penned emotion.
The distance made no difference
In terms of precious moments spent together in love's kind embrace
That spanned from here to that harsh place
To Afghan air from English chair.
The depth of feeling so revealing, thoughts
Of him, through thick and thin I'd write supporting
And reporting happy things from life back home where his
Thoughts would often roam.
When times were hard for him to bear, when loneliness would
Bring despair and minimise shut networks down, I'd ease his frown with
Letters that still got to him despite the circumstances grim.
That's when the ink of love worked best
When camp morale was so depressed
He'd tell the lads don't be distressed look at the stars
Towards the West where our letters are addressed.
The ink of love can transcend parting
Words of hope and pride were starting something quite remarkable
Within a place despicable. The letters are a ray of light within the
Soul that glows so bright when ink of love is used to write.
Write everyday to those who stay on foreign soil & don't delay,
For they depend on those who send the priceless ink of love to spend,
Repaid ten times at their tour end.

The Man In The Corner.

Anon

Just the boring old fart in the corner
As you young ones no doubt will perceive
He's old, he's done nowt
He's poor, he'd got nowt
But what he's seen, you would never believe.

Just the boring old fart in the corner
Keeps on talking, but says not a lot
Just keeps rattling on
Like an old machine gun
Do you hear what he says? Not a jot.

Just the boring old fart in the corner
Who saw all his mates shot to shreds
Mates so proud and so tall
Mates who gave up their all
So you kids could sleep safe in your beds.

Just the boring old fart in the corner
Whose memories now just seem to fade.
Is his mind playing games,
Can't remember their names.
Was it Michael or Johnson or Wade?

Just the boring old fart in the corner
Whose life has been touched by a war
Is his mind filled with rage
Or has time made him sage,
Or can he be bothered no more.

Just the boring old fart in the corner,
Go over and buy him a drink.
He's the reason, you see
Why you stand there so free
Go and listen, it might make you think.

Soldier's Creed

Eddie Dee Williams (youtube.com/clevarval58)

Hero Soldier's Wounded Warrior's
Hero Soldier's Wounded Warrior's

Land Liberty I pledge to thee
Never ever quit or ever retreat
Stand ready destroy the enemy
Close combat, defending country
Men women in the military
Mean lean fighting machines
Sustain battle scared injuries
Down with the Soldier's Creed

Say you people help our Heroes
Say you people help our Heroes
Say you people help our Heroes
Say you people help our Heroes

I'm an American Soldier
From a team of highly trained Warrior's
My Country Tis of Thee
Mission First, Never Accepting Defeat
Men Women in the Military
Shield America from the enemy
Battle injuries line of duty
Upholding Soldier's Creed

Say you people help our heroes
Hero Soldiers, Wounded Warriors
Say you people help our heroes
Say you Americans help our guardian's
Say you Americans help our Veteran's

It's Different kind of mission
Transitioning back into Civilian
Thank you for the sacrifice
Defending America's way of life
Freedom doesn't come easily
Men Women Military casualties
From Shore to shore from sea to sea
Thank you for serving long live Soldier's Creed

The Letter

By C. Brooks

Jack had enlisted
When the dreaded message came
It read Captain Christian
Badly injured in a raid.

Pouring sweat & weeping
Weeping silently
All Jack kept repeating
Was Dad, oh Dad, just hang on please.

When he reached the bedside
The man he idolized
His best friend & mentor
Was to pay the highest price
Then on the brink of heaven
Jack's hand he tried to find
& from his fingers fell the letter
To my son, the true light of my eyes.

"I risked my life
For the greatest cause
& was proud to be part of it all
I've loved my job
You'll love your's
And you'll have no regrets son, I'm sure
I know you'll march on
For the sake of peace
And pin your faith on freedom
The way my son, you pinned your faith on me".

Missing You

September 5, 2010 C. Lloy

It's late at night our little girl is here
She has your eyes and your smile
I've seen your face, in my dreams a million times
I tell our little one, we'll see you in a while

Oh I'm missing you, things haven't been the same
I thank you for your service, I'm glad to have your name
Oh I'm missing you, I pray day and night
That God will bring you safely in my arms to hold you tight

The months go by, I've counted every day
That you've been gone, fighting to be free
Some people hate, they don't seem to understand
What freedom costs to live in this great land

And I'm missing you, things haven't been the same
How I wish there was a way to shield me from this pain?
Oh I'm missing you, you've really made me proud
Fighting for our freedom so we don't live without

I carry my phone on me so I don't miss your call
I miss you so much baby I can't think at all

And we're missing you, things haven't been the same
We won't take for granted, America, this land
We will hold you tight, we may never let you go
When you're safely in our arms, safely back at home,
We're missing you

Newport Waters

By Robert .M. Sorensen

Girl, do you have a message that lasts?
I sent you mine, will you buy mine back?
Do you have a reply, is it "maybe", or "yes"?
Can you relate to my rhyme? I know your caress.
Don't send me no "note in a bottle", no ocean...
Can reach my long distance number.
You'll get no recorder, I want you back...
More than ever.

I walk through skyscrapers blazing in my dreams.
You're the princess that bleeds and screams.
Cold as icing, a re-run of "sweet sixteen".
A top the Twin Towers on a religious holiday,
Unable to reach Heaven's Gates in May.
Want to touch my fire without getting burned,
I'm the sphinx at High Noon.

Before the sun sets & Liberty's torch is extinguished,
I'll rescue you from high altitude reaches.

It's now, or never, it's red, not black.
I'm yours forever, you're my princess in silver leather.
As New York begins to crumble,
Let me escort you to NewportWaters,
Our yacht will soar to the cosmic borders.

Lance Coporal Tyler Christopher with fiancee Katie Cherrette.

Tyler is tougher than a taliban bomb

By Joe Christopher

Him tougher dan a Taliban bomb,
Tougher dan a Taliban bomb.
Dem blow up me son
Dem Taliban man,
Wid dem eye ee dee
And shittie bottie
But 'im tougher dan a Taliban bomb.

Him a still de strong
And you cant go wrong
Check out me song
'Cause 'im British army
& de British army
Mek dem tougher dan a Taliban bomb

Lagar in dem hand,
See dem still stand,
Frenchie by 'im side
Mek 'im ano blushinga bride.
Look 'pon de rifles
Eating trifles
Dance 'pon barb wire,
Pants on fire,
Sing like choir,
And tuffer dan a Taliban bomb

Hear de people say
When de come out play,
Jigging in dem combats
Pissed as wombats
And Tougher Dan A Taliban bomb

My soldier comrade

By Pauline Barnes

My head is propped up on a rock
Tho, drifting in & out,
I`m thinking I am lucky
To be here-right now!
My heads concealed
My arms concealed
My legs & body too,
The whole of me is shielded...
In the battered arms of you!...

An ode to our beloved politicians

By Marie – Germany

So a mole has exposed the greedy rats
Labour, Tory & some Democrats
All found with noses deep in the trough
The lads the cads & the Grandee toffs.

Some noses go deeper - so the more they scoff
Like a claim for a mortgage – that's already paid off
Cleaning moats & chandeliers
This vile contempt brings a soul to tears.

It's not my fault the rodents plead
Whilst drowning in their unfettered greed
A hornet's nest of thieves and crooks
One by one must be brought to book.

No fighting between the Lords & lads
'Cos each one of them is equally as bad
Barristers and lawyers – ah! ...now we know why
Each one well trained in the fine art of lies.

My second home has a mind of its own
I woke up one morning and found it had flown
It just keeps on flipping backwards & forth
I bought it in London – then POW! – it moved up north.

I get so confused with all the houses I've used
And for what purpose I quite often muse
I did have a flat – I can remember that
I sold for profit – 'cos I wanna be a big fat cat.

A family member appears on the pay roll
With a rent free abode – the lucky ol' soul
One house on my exes will just never do
And because I could – I claimed for two.

Remembrance Day – he laid down a wreath
Never considering what lay there beneath
While people shed tears & remembered the dead
'I'm quite out of pocket' spun in his head.

A scandalous deed & shame on this nation
To claim back the money for a church donation
How low can one stoop - it's such a disgrace
But his Maker one day he will have to face.

Don't they know they appear uncouth?
When sat on your telly bending the truth
With an assassin's grin and glassy eyes
Dirty little piggies telling such porky-pies.

The rules are flawed and were all doomed to fail
& we don't belong in a rotten old jail
The system is broke so I'm not to blame
Though I'll never pay back all the money I've claimed.

A sad error of judgement they'll have us believe
When months in the planning with intent to deceive
They bend all the rules until they've succeeded
A crooked accountant is all that is needed.

Some dodge paying tax using taxpayer's cash
And defend their actions so bold & so brash
Christmas decorations & cute Teddy Bears
Knives & forks and some nice earthenware.

All my chums were complaining of wet feet
When playing tennis as one of my treats
A pipe had burst beneath the tennis court
Oh I'll claim that on expenses – so I thought.

And that snooty old fool who came out to drool
And say we're all jealous of his big house and pool
So deeply disturbing & so plainly immoral
&...it looks nothing at all like Balmoral.

Someone must do my gardening for me
Cutting my grass - & chopping down trees
Let's not forget the cheating louse
Who wangled some money to buy a duck house.

We need butlers, gardeners & cleaners
To this end there are no misdemeanours
Someone must do it I'm sure you'll agree
I'm just plain crazy – and my wife is so lazy -you see.

Oh I'm a fool with sloppy accounting
A pathetic excuse as the pressure was mounting
He thought he could pickpocket the nation at will
But caught like a sneak-thief with hands in the till.

They knock your door, smile & say
You'll vote for me on next polling day
I'll fight for you & your family
Honest to God I'm not in this for me.

Stifle that giggle & hide your grin
And resist the punch upon the chin
Dishonourable folks - the butt of new jokes
Reputations all mangled, strangled - & broke.

Please God don't say that integrity has died
Just because cheap-shots duped & lied
You know too well good people exist
They're just so hard to find in this murky ol' mist.

The winter of 1944

By Lt. Norman Harris (13corps movement control)

Remembering the hills North of Florence.
The winter of 44
Was spent mostly outdoor
Because of the war
No Italian sun
Just the sound of a gun
Fired by the Hun
Snow, mud & rain
Give us a pain
Perhaps we'll be dry
Bye & bye.

If rations appear
We'll be full of good cheer
But snow halts all
& faces fall
But Johnnie Indian comes near
& Compos appears
With sugar, milk and tea
Three cheers for the 5th Indian
We give with great glee.

The fallen are greeted

Jenny Barnes

The line of cars
March slowly past
The graven crowds
Dressed in black
Their respect to bestow as
The fallen are greeted with flowers
Red roses thrown
From gloved fingers
Numbed with cold
But the grief will last
For longer than even the children
May ever know.

Spread with the flag of the
United Kingdom
Their caps of honour
Adorn their coffins
As one after the other
They return home
To their loved ones
We pray they rest
In peace at last
For the desert has taken them
In fearful blasts
God bless our soldiers
Home at last.

Yet there is hope
For in weeks
Or months to come
Their comrades in arms
Will march past
Those who have grieved
Their thoughts
With friends in arms
Whom they have lost.

Black rose

By Alan Mckean

A single black rose
On a mound of fresh earth
Is all that is left
To mark
A proud uniform.

A hole in a fmaily
An empty chair
A folded flag
A coloured ribbon
A circle of metal.

A single black rose.

The naked goddess

By Darrell .Keith Harris

Her love is pure,
No worries no fret-face.
Like an angel's body
Built for sin -
Her course is
Definitely, win win -
Her Heart is big
Her skin is soft -
Her face so pretty
My words got lost -
She wanted to save
The world you see -
The Naked Goddess
Loves humanity.

Love is safe

By Rosalind Doherty

Love is safe
Love is real
Love is everything to heal
Love will protect you
Love will surround you
Love is everything you feel
Love brings hope
Love brings peace
Love is safe.

Cyberspace war

By Jeannette Slavinski

The Cyberspace War,
Became an Intergalatic Battle
Between Facebook seekers & oppressors.
The Naked Goddess had created
A fortress of opportunity,
For those willing to express their ability
Indebted to armed forces.
From far & wide an armitage
Of tongues reverberated,
An organic verbose Armeggeddon,
Threatening, demanding, nihalating,
The spit was venemous.
Mankind had formed war online. Star Wars.
But love & metal sustained
The fortress core, &
Finally the deserters pressed the destruct button.
Words not weapons, won The Cyberspace War.

72.8% water

By Arturo Rhodes

The person you love is 72.8% water
You can drink them in a glass
Gargle them in the bathroom mirror
Draw a heart & arrow in the steam
Snorkle to the depths with silver fins
Climb into a divers suit with leaded boots
Walk the depths a phone line to the shore
Crawl on your hands & knees across the sand
Your love evaporating to form a mirage
That wobbles along the horizon
Loveless and waterless you stumble into a bar
Order drinks and suck up a long straw
Take a short stub pencil then begin this
Rhymless rhyme....The person you love is 72.8% water.

Battle harvest

By Chloe Honeyborne

Shadowed face. Trudges turning,
Curving, discerning, trenched trails
Cut. Into hard earth.
Routes rooted, widening unknown
No-Man's land loomed:
Battered and blighted, beaten and `bited`
Foddered knees sway
From whence the flower bloomed.

Whats in a voice

By Emma Louise Heaver

A voice can control a million bombs
Peace in time will come
A voice can lead a man to war
A shrill impatient sound that leads to more.
A voice can signify defeat
& young lives increase the score.
Whats in a voice?
A voice demands the final time
And leads to losses that speak no more.
Whats in a voice?

The Freedom Tree

(Love from a tree from me to thee)
By William Ferguson

Unable to move with only a trail to see
A wounded warrior's spirit trapped inside a tree
Eyes fixed on an approaching girl that has potential
She may be the one that's providential
A little tin box lies hidden beneath my roots
Kicked open accidently by her boots
Inside she finds a letter & a wooden key
The letter from my heart which exposes me
I feel her back pressed against my bark
As I drop down leaves around her in this forgotten park
She opens the letter & begins to read
Of a person torn of war desperately in need
Her name ghostly appears at the top
Scaring her but she cannot stop
Dear April, keep it always & remember me
The wounded soldier inside this tree
She caresses me & replaces the tin
And I start to grow another wooden key within.

Mark's soldier son, Luke

By D.L.Taylor

Today, Mark can wear a smile,
For his soldier son is safe awhile,
No more worry from each news report.
One day will it be him is your sad thought.

With every war filled day,
No one can express the pain of war
When it knocks at a your young sons door,
But, today Mark can smile.

For God is good, Luke's safe and free
Away from the torment & misery,
Of battles cruel on this day, made each time
His pals step on a dreaded mine.

So keep those moments close to your heart
When the next young soldiers have to part
From family, the friends anew
It could be you -

But today, Mark can wear a smile -
His loving son is safe awhile.

No peace today

By Donna Mahon

Another blast, let's run & see!
I see the smoke, I smell the steel.
"Get down from there!" My mother roars,
"It isn't safe..............there may be more".
& then the shots ring out so loud,
"Lie on the floor.........don't make a sound".

The sirens blare, the people shout;
"A bomb, a bomb! Get out, Get out!"
With a child in arms, I run so fast
Around the corner, and then....the blast.
My life, our home, where to from here?
Slow motion, silence fills the air.

"I just want peace". My mother said,
"Too many hurt, too many dead!"
Too many years, the river flows
Through bloody fields, heartbroken homes.
Dear God please make it go away,
My mother says, "No peace today".

A Narrative poem on Meeting Clint Eastwood

You raise me up

By Jeannette Slavinski

DAY 1

You walked in Tall so Tall
Into the secret gem
To the treasured rhythm of
A Million Dollar Baby.
As the waves parted
I held me breath,
As each and everyone felt your prowess
& clapped to the sway of your diagonal walk,
An unshakable sapphire focus
Greeting me fondly,
As the beat 'o' my heart beat
Will he won't he will he won't will he won't he like me.
I apologised for not knowing the tune
Of the Russian pianist
I had not seen the film,
I`m not a film buff you see
But you smiled very warmly.
In your presence I heard your voice
For the very first time,
I could hardly lift my glass
To toast the ruby wine
It barely touched my lips.
Trembling with excitement & nerves
You picked up the verve
& your arm curved around me like a wing.
Breaking the ice,
You asked where I lived.
Shakily I replied, "Manchester".
"Aaaaaah Manchester." Your accent sighed
That tingled up my spine.
Is this real thought I, only me,
"South Manchester Cheshire actually
Lewis Carroll's Mad Hatter

Alice in Wonderland territory
I feel like Alice cheers to your health"
Phew! I said in one breath
A nod and a laugh reassured me a friend.

DAY 2

Drat I can't play golf I exclaimed!
So came the tour,
Of the residents gym to keep slim
And an intro to
Cool Hand Hosea (Luke),
Who dropped me down-town
In the famed pick-up, without orangatang! -
Carmel by the Sea -
A Hamlet with wide ocean gates
A rumba tide
Swirling, Reptunium spays
Heady cypress lined lanes
Musky pine cones arranged
Gingerbread cottages
Toot sweet to eat
And Tor House, A
Craggy stone love stone tower
I nick name Hansel & Gretel,
Streets with no names
But plenty of fame
And a nestled Forest Theatre
Baptised,
Where the stars never die
I tell no lie
I was born under a wandering star,
Twelth Night shines so bright.
Its incense puts one in a trance
As the Mission Bell peals,
On a whispering breeze
Come join the dance -
It's surreal.
The warren waltzes with life
Its citizens seem quite mellow.
English tea shops serving jam tarts,
Antiques & galleries filled with fine art,
Imbued with the law of a famed Mayor,
California is big Carmel is quite small
The longer I walk it seems to get smaller and smaller!

The Naked Goddess - Love & War

Spinning, spinning I'm now spinning into a ginnel,
Alongside a gifted white feather,
Hey presto, I'm in the heart of Carmel.
The lane was skewiff with second hand books
One almost had to stand on ones head to take a look,
There were plays & poetry galore
North American history -
PowWow, its making me dizzy
Amidst the maze
No maps either in the haze
In case I got lost,
No rush, hush hussssssssssh,
It's a sleepy hollow.
Slowly, sloooooowly my trust
Led me to an Eden
Enchantingly beating,
A wishing well stood in full view
No need of a dime or of a rhyme
This fairy tale had come true.
There were tinkling chimes, prickly cacti,
Offerings of symbols of peace,
Sweet smelling roses galore
A rusting key to a door,
Unlocked, unchained I entered,
Elevated am I, blessed & bound
Golly gosh, now I'd found –
The Secret Garden.

My Mexican friends to meet me at three
Barefoot I sat on the side
Reflective of my luck & life.
Through the corner of my eye I saw the
`Crown Royal`
Glide by, next thing I know
A hands reaching for me -
As Clint raises me up graciously.
Without further A do he opened the door,
I stepped in the back in surprise & in awe
Driven by Clint at the wheel,
Crickey I'm in a whirl scene once more &
The car, purred along like the cat that'd got the cream.
The looking glass glance makes me feel
Rather coy – in Clint's glint I see a boy,

Eye's soft and inquiring -
He asked, "How was my day, what did I see?"
To which I answered with glee, "I found,
The Secret Garden"
Then sharing the joy in my soul,
He smiled with a sigh "Aaaaaaaaaah,
"The Secret Garden".
Back at the ranch I'm still in a trance
Spell bound by my new world mystique,
Mission farm is a balm from Carmel's dance
My soles are quite sore
So I decide to perch on a pumpkin,
"Clint your harvest are huge" I laugh out quite loud,
"May be I'll go to the ball, now where is fairy God Mother?
Amused at my comment Clint laughs again and again
The American dream, Clint's farming & livin -
Next offer, I'm invited to stay for Thanksgivin.
Yum yum my first taste of pumpkin pie thought I,
Good health to the voluptuous vine.
Thank you my dear Clint, I'd love to never go away -
But I'm committed to feed the homeless next day.

DAY 3

Its brief, alas too bad, farewells are so sad,
The turkey is basting, Santa Monica is calling.
This dream child is real for young & for old
My Carmelite prayer now has been told.
I'm inspired by Mayor Clint's values & charm
Carmel's captured my passion my love
Good gracious I'm hooked.
Mission Ranch is a rock
Clint Eastwoods story book
Filled with fairytales forever & ever
Its welcoming magic I experienced first hand
An odyssey a heroic fantasy some may think.
My fortune is shared for you & for all
In pen & in ink.
I'll be back, I did say
Wild horses or dragons wont keep me away
Abracadabra
Then with a puff & a siiiiiiiiiiiiiiiigh - Kissssssssssed
The blessed - Cornerstone - Goodbye

I am called a friend

By Thunder Spirit Cooper

When you are lonely and despair
Has come to knock on your door
And you know its there,
Just waiting for you to let it in,
& you try to send your mind
To another place & time
Of happy memories, but your
Heart feels heavy & you feel weak
The dark shadows start to creep
Into your heart, your soul, your spirit
Your very being. Remember me
For I am called a friend,
And I will be there to hold your hand.

Tranquil

By Mr. Anderton

Walking down a quiet country lane,
Helps to keep you sane not insane.

Over the sty & along the stream,
Drifting along in a dream.

Watching the seagulls following the plough,
While blackbirds sings off a bough.

But those who take no heed are,
Wrapped up in a world full of war & greed.

The tranquillity is all around,
For those whose feet stay on the ground.

For this Dream

By Danson Cruise

I sought not to find
In those past dreams
A love I had to invent.
My heart beat in solitude
Beneath the uniform of a soldier,
Whilst circulating a name
On cupids arrow to call you.
But I see that you arrive
Equally in time for this dream,
That will never end.

Loneliness

By Mendo Henriques

There is nothing so sad
As loneliness...
It is the home of despair
The house of the poor
The bride of the mad
A disease with no cure
The wife of myself
The lover of hell
And the angel of death.

All would be blissful
& everyone shining
If there were no loneliness...
The fragrance of being
Would come to us
If it only disappeared......

Alas, at the end of the day
It comes again & again
With merciful blindness
& I stay alone with thee,
loneliness.

Who am I

By M. W. Domeretsky

He who is fixed on a star does not change his mind.
From my thoughts I remember this all too well in my life.
Those who come, will come again, Those who don`t, will wish they had.
Meaning, those who come and stop in to understand me will
Understand who I am,
And what I`m made of. Those who come, will come again.

Free Spirit

By Randell Crow

It`s a spirited move..
That a free spirit makes...
Like the wind in the trees...
Or the ground when it quakes...
It`s a spirited path...
That her free spirit goes...
Down the trails in my life...
Through the fields past the Hollows...
Up through the mountains & on to the sea...
Her gentle free spirit is running with me...
I can look in her eyes...
And feel her heart beat...
Syncopation, Rhythm...From the ground `neath my feet...
Her dance is like that of the wind & the rain...
There for you to love...
But not to contain...
So put away your cages, chains, bars & your walls...
`Cause she`s on the move...
When she hears the calls...
Of the wind in the trees...
And the ground when it shakes...
It`s a spirited move.....
That a Free Spirit makes.

Clint Eastwood

Anonomous

Clint is our handsome Rawhide,
Loved by his fans worldwide.
Instantly recognizable as a mega star,
Nobody knew about his war,
That place far from our shore.

Eastwood a veteran of the Korean War,
Always standing behind our forces.
Strong the image he enforces.
The characters he acts, fight for right,
With passion as well as might.
On behalf of "Help for Heroes" that you supported,
On behalf of the book you helped plan,
Dreamers & poets thank an Action Man.

So strong is my heart

By Recardo Patrick
(Recardo had a No 1 hit with Sad Sweet Dreamer)

So strong is my heart

Although we are apart
I will never wain,
In the long lasting love
That I have for you.

While fighting this war
sometimes not being sure
Of what we are doing,
But we will see it through.

My mind is strong
for right or for wrong.
These battles we will fight,
with no matter how long.

Moving across the fields

By David Berrisford

Moving across fields of red & red,
The ghosts of the Somme warily tread,
By now they should be in paradise,
But they still suffer the mud & the flys & the lice,
Dawn light glints on a threatening barb,
In a million miles of wire,
Nothing but the smell of the rot & the piss & the fire,
What made this piece of France,
Chosen seemingly by chance,
The best spot for a tactical advance?
They've been advancing under orders since 1917,
They're not sure what happened in between,
The pit of the stomach has a feeling of dread ,
Maybe this once was a corn field,
Now it lies dead,
Distant voices of rememberance services in their ears,
But of course that came in later years,
For now they have to experience their demise afresh,
Tangled in the barb wire mesh,
Corned beef for lunch with bread an dread,

Sweet child of mine

By Jeannette Slavinski

Sweet child of mine,
Red bows bedeck velvet brown hair
Cascading upon marbled shoulders.
Cupid lipp'd, almond green eyes,
Ghost of a father in her placid stare,
Porcelein skin translucently bright,
Enigmatic smile to beguile.
Whole universe at your feet,
You are a mere shadow of war-Neutral territory...
His law, He'd fractured
Coz he'd stained the love
We had made,& incarcerated her in
A barbed wire cage!

Young poet laureate

WORLD BOOK DAY

The Naked Goddess receives an invite on World Book Day to Byrchall High School, Wigan.

Is it love?

By Gemma Jones

Is it love I was wondering
When your heart sounds like its thundering,
Or when my stomach starts to flutter
& my heart melts like hot butter,
Is it love?

Is it love when you get goosebumps all over
Or is it just a Casanova,
Or is it when he whispers in your ear
The words you've always wanted to hear?

It is love in many ways
When you walk round in a daze?
That is what you call love,
So come give us a kiss & hug.

Time has stopped

**By Madeline Roche, Aged 14,
Cardinal Langley R.C High School pupil**

The love I feel,
The pain he felt.
No time can heal,
His presence I smelt.

My heart is broke,
His heart has stopped,
The shock did choke,
My stomach dropped.

This poppy I wear,
As a sign of hope,
I promise, I swear,
For your sake I'll cope.

Not yet worried about the years,
You were in your prime.
Flow will the tears,
Pass will the time.

From me, you were taken,
One in a million, bespoke.
Convinced they were mistaken,
Or playing some sick joke.

Without you, I am nothing.
A jigsaw, incomplete.
Gone, my everything,
Now, just a blank sheet.

They say there's a reason for everything,
Well maybe this was for the best,
The way you went, not the timing,
Instead of suffering that awful cancer, located in your chest.
When I took my vows I meant them,
"In sickness & in health".

Nothing more important to me than you, not one person, item,
Nothing else mattered to me, not possessions, not wealth.
& now, I'm left without you,
Never will I forget, forever I will cherish.
Your bravery will always shine through,
For your sake, sad memories I shall banish.

I wish

By Kimberley Purvis (age 14yrs)

I wish the war would finish.
I wish that we were in peace.
I wish the guns & shells would stop.
I wish that war would cease.

Why can`t the world be right?
Why so we have to fight?
Why can`t I be in front of a warm fire
Instead of in the line of fire?

Every night I pray
That tomorrow will be the day
When the war stops
When the treaty is signed
When we can go back home.

Bang, bang

By Daniel Fitzpatrick, Byrchall High School, Wigan

Bang, bang the flares are striked,
Lighting up the skies in the night.
The men are scared, fright after fright,
Planes are flying as high as kites.
So please support our willing troops,
As they go down in massive groups,
The families are shocked, the families are scared,
Some men come back with nothing but a blare.

'I will remember them'

By a 14 year old girl

Who are these men who march so proud,
Who quietly weep, eyes closed, head bowed.
These are the men who once were boys,
Who missed out on youth and all of it's joys.

Who are these men with aged faces,
Who silently count the empty spaces.
These are the men who gave their all,
Who fought for their country for freedom for all.

Who are these men with sorrowful look,
Who still can remember the lives that were took.
These are the men who saw young men die,
The price of freedom is always high.

Who are the men in the midst of pain,
Whispered comfort to those they would not see again.
These are the men whose hands held tomorrow,
Who brought back our future with blood, tears, and sorrow.

Who are these men who promise to keep,
Alive in their hearts the ones God holds asleep.
These are the men to whom I promise again,
Veterans, my friends, 'IWILL REMEMBER THEM'

The final cry

By Jake Manchester Year 7, Byrchall High, Wigan

Just me & just two rounds,
Even I can hear my own heart pound.
Aiming down my scope,
Lying down on that damp slope.
Guns being fired,
Bombs being blown,
Hands full of blood and not my own.
Nothing but a solitary rose,
I'll be dead soon everyone knows.

I stand up from cover,
Head held high.
I huff, I puff and let out a loud sigh.
Up raises my gun,
Firing all my enemies dropping with a thud.
One by one,
Shoot them all with my gun.
Then, without time to think,
A grenade comes over and blows before I can blink.

Luckily I survive,
But maybe next time I may not be so lucky,
Risk my own every day to save another life.

In the war

By Georgia Snape, Byrchall High School, Wigan

They sacrifice their lives for us, as they fight in the fields of dust.
The gun shots in the air are so bright, as they fight through the gloomy night.
Everywhere is noise, noise is everywhere, through the big bang & blur.
The families & friends that have always cared

Their love can no longer be shared
The dead soldiers can fight no more, as they lay there on the floor.
Families pray for the lives that have been lost, which were not worth the cost.

The heroes

By Ashlea Rooney, Byrchall High School, Wigan

The heroes stood line by line
Waiting for that dreadful time,
As they save themselves from death
We wait hoping for the best,
While the soldiers fall to the floor
Stop the fighting, please, no more,
Be grateful for what we have today
Otherwise we wouldn't be living this way,
They saved our country they saved us all
Now we stand proud and tall.

The truth hurts

By Rebecca Tickle, Byrchall High School, Wigan

Lies, lies, lies they thought as they strolled down
From the little mountain far about a mile from town.
Clutching all objects one in each hand
As their mucky, big boots clashed between the sand.

Bang, bang, bang they heard from a far distance away
As the little town they'd once called home was quickly shipped from bay.
Down, down, down they plunged into the cold and dark pit
Like a fox just been shot to death or a window just been hit.

Boom, boom, boom they saw as dirt arose to the sky
As one by one they went from the trench waiting & prepared to die.
Lies, lies, lies they once said as the poppies lie in bloom
As the soldiers lie in sleep now from that dark, crimson doom.

Boom, boom, boom

By Terry Merritt, Byrchall High School, Wigan

Boom, boom, boom,
The flowers begin to bloom.
In summer it rains,
As they fight in vain.
In autumn they shoot,
As we travel on foot.
In winter there's snow,
Christmas here we go,
They say fight we say no.

In spring I lie,
As I'm about to die.
War is brutal,
You cannot trust,
Run away if you must.

War, war

By Tom Neil, Byrchall High School, Wigan

War, war should be never more
It's tight on people & cruel
War, war should be never more
It kills all those that are good
War, war should be never more
It's pointless & it's sad
War, war should be never more
If you know what's good for you
War, war should be never more
Now and in the future

Bang! crash! gush! scream!

By Leonnie Myers, Byrchall High School, Wigan

BANG! Went the bombs

CRASH! Went the buildings

GUSH! From the blood

SCREAM! From the people

BANG! Went the guns

CRASH! Went the planes

GUSH! From the seas

SCREAM! From the people

BANG! Went the towns

CRASH! Went the souls

GUSH! Went the lives

SCREAM! From the people

BANG! CRASH! GUSH! SCREAM!

We will win

By Jonathon Johnson, Byrchall High School, Wigan

As I walked pass all my friends,
My love I send.

The bombs drop,
Bullets pop,
Shells fly,
I could die.

My mates are helping,
Push the fight,
I am only thinking is it right.

WE WILL WIN,
We will fight,
I'm just hoping this is right.

I miss you

By Jade Wilson, Byrchall High School, Wigan

I miss you...
I know I need to remember you...
To make the days go by.
Sometimes I can't help but sigh.
But I know I will see you soon.
Maybe next year we'll be on our honeymoon.
But either way it doesn't matter.
Soon it will end.

...

I miss you

x x x

10

By Shannon Fitzgerald, Byrchall High School, Wigan

The soldiers are fighting boys & men,
The survivors will be not many more than just ten.
As they are all dying throughout the day,
These are the months March, April & May.
Now that the solders are gone,
The poppies start to grow one by one.
& family & friends will see no more,
Their loved ones that once walked through the door.

In my heart forever

By Gemma Beesley, Byrchall High School, Wigan

The air was filled with thick, black smoke.
Two years ago he had left home.
Those two years he had been walking, walking, walking,
Clutching weapons in his hands with all his might,
Their boots trudged through the mud,
Foot prints left there to symbolise the soldiers.

Suddenly a bang was heard from a distance further away,
Heads turned,
Hearts thudded with absolute dread,
Another attack was underway.

Bang,
As a solider turned around, another snipers bullet was aimed,
The solider crashed to the ground,
Motionless, breathless.

The enemy retired to the camps,
Another day had gone by,
The dead lay there peacefully,
Although they come and go,
They will always be known,
In Flanders fields.

Love for the people

By Josh Passey, Byrchall High School, Wigan

Love for those people in the cold & the wind,
Forgive those people, who have died & have sinned,
Love for those people who wear their heart on their sleeve,
Love for the families who have been wounded & grieve
On the front line body's drop,
All of the fighting just needs to stop,
Love for the men who cry & whimper,
Who risk there lives in summer & winter.

Togetherness

By Daniel Simpson, Byrchall High School, Wigan

Wanting
Ache
Revenge
Patriotic
Officer
Executed
Torn
Rifles
Young
Destruction
Envey
Alone
Togetherness
Hurting

Soldiers rights

By Alex Jackson, Byrchall High School, Wigan

We all have our rights
So we're told
Our future is bright
Theirs is cold

Then I fall

By Zac Cullen, Byrchall High School, Wigan

The bullets radiated off trees,
Running for an age,
Then the cry of a fallen man,
Another & another,
They fall again & again,
The bullets coming ever so closer,
Bang bang the chatter of machine gunfire,
Then I fall,
The ground rushes up too meet me,
& everything goes dark.

I miss you so

By Charlotte Wilson, Byrchall High School, Wigan

Like Flanders flow
Waiting for this day to end.

Keep singing sweet
Until we meet
Waiting for this day to end.

I know it breaks your heart
With us being apart
Waiting for this day to end.

I'll see you soon
Upon the skies
Waiting for the day to end.

My friend

By Nathan O'Keefe, Byrchall High School, Wigan

My friend had died,
By my side,
Covered in blood,
Amongst the mud,
Behind the wire,
Was all that fire,
To do what's right,

My baby jack

By Sophie Dews, Byrchall High School, Wigan

He walked out the door two long years ago,
Big & proud fighting like so,
Waiting, waiting for his return,
Not long now I say.
Knowing he's a million miles away,
I dream that he is ok.

I tell myself he'll be ok,
But I know it will not take the pain away,
Listening to the radio every day,
Hoping & praying in every way,
It's not his day today,
Every time the door bell goes, I think it's them,
Coming to tell the news he's dead.

But still I wait day after day,
Watching as the people pray,
A miracle happens,
For me it's different now I got him back,
My son, my child,
My Baby jack.

In Africa

By Joram Mutuzabi

It is our wish
It is our dream
Our wish to leave
Our dream to survive
You dream to have a mother
Your dream came true
She`s there for you
My people are dying
Dying young lives
My people on earth
The earth being the mother
The earth being a relative of a loved one
In Africa my continent
The soil has closed our parents & friends faces
& the soil has now become my toil
The soil has become a relative & freind
Who is going to stand by me
Circumstances destroyed my sister
I was left alone
Without a shoulder to lean on
All the people want is a life
I thank God for life
I thank God for my mother
I thank God for my grandmother
Lets have peace in Africa.

Cold stone

By Jemma-Louise Cowen aged 13

Why do I wait here?
Upon a cold stone floor?
Why wish that you are near,
When I know that you're no more.

What torment doth enthral me?
That I've so heartfully deserved.
Is this hard cruel path my destiny?
Is this pain for me reserved?

In this harsh desolate world,
Does one single star shine in hope?
That one day peace & kindness be unfurled,
That in unity mankind will cope.

Will one day a sun rise?
And bring happiness and hope to this Earth?
Will a single beauty open my eyes?
Show me this planets true worth.

But till then I wait here,
Upon a cold stone floor.
And wish that you are near,
When I know that you're no more.

Last but not least

From the bottom of my heart a sincere thank you for choosing to read this anthology. I hope you've enjoyed the heartfelt penmanship within. The Naked Goddess continues to flourish please stay posted to her web.

Love & Light

JX
The Naked Goddess

THE
naked
GODDESS

TEMPTATIONS

Coming January 2013

www.thenakedgoddess.com

A reality anthology "for the people by the people"